Contents

Living or non-living?

I believe our biggest problem is the same biggest issue that the whole world is facing, and that's* habitat *destruction.

Steve Irwin, wildlife warrior (1962–2006)

The world is made up of living and non-living things. The homes we live in, city buildings, furniture, clothes and toys are all non-living things. Even some things from nature, such as water, rocks and sand, are non-living.

Living things are all around us, too. They are on mountains, in forests, in the ocean, in deserts – even in our backyards.

Living things all have certain things in common. Scientists group living things together based on what they look like and how they behave.

Sometimes living things become **endangered** or even **extinct**. We should all look after our planet so that living things have a better chance of surviving.

Did you know?
A blue whale's heart is as big as a car. An ant can carry up to 50 times its own body weight. And some plants actually eat meat.

habitat the natural environment of a living thing
endangered a species of animal or plant that is close to dying out
extinct a species of animal or plant that has died out

Everything in the world is either living or non-living.

LET'S FIND OUT

- What is a living thing?
- What do living things need to stay alive?
- What is a life cycle?
- How are living things alike? How are they different?
- Why are some living things endangered?

What's a living thing?

Everything in the world is either living or non-living. All living things have certain **characteristics** that are the same.

Living things have cells

All living things are made up of cells. A cell is very small – it can only be seen under a **microscope**. A cell has water in it, as well as other materials.

Some living things, such as **bacteria**, are made up of just one cell. Other living things are made up of many, many cells. All the cells work together to keep the living thing alive.

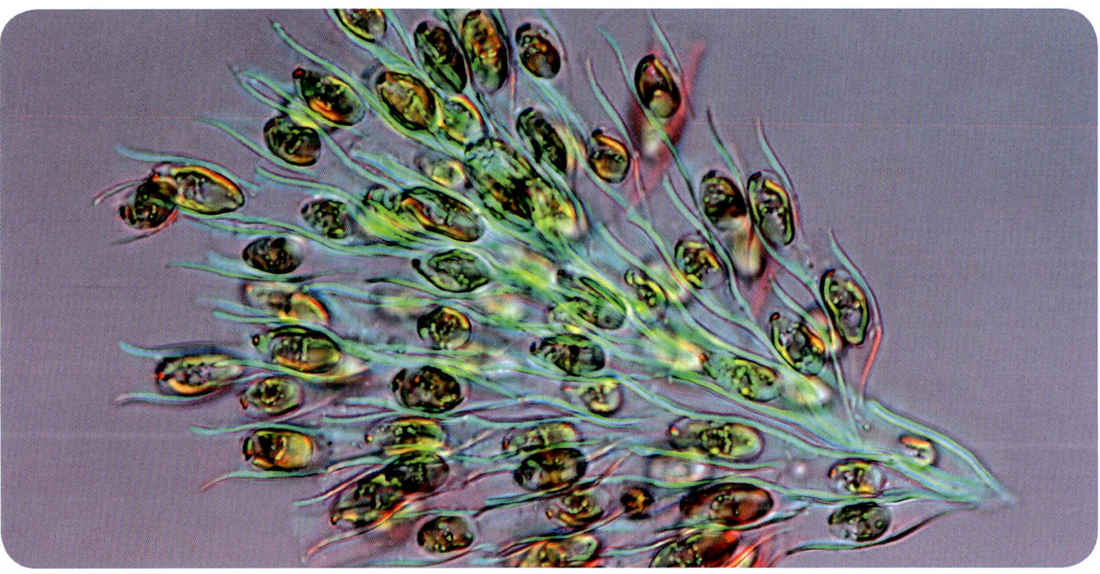

Cells seen from under a microscope

characteristics the features or qualities of a thing
microscope a machine used to see very tiny things
bacteria tiny, single-celled living things that can only be seen under a microscope

Living things grow

All living things grow. Most living things begin small and grow until they become an adult. Some living things begin their lives looking like their parents, but are much smaller, such as many bugs.

A monkey and its baby look alike.

Other living things look quite different to their parents. They grow and change over time to become an adult. For example, a tadpole changes into a frog when it becomes an adult.

Living things respond

All living things respond to things around them. They react to **stimuli** such as touch, light, heat and smell. For example, the leaves of some plants droop in the heat, a cat purrs when you pat it and a person squints in bright light.

This puffer fish responds to danger by puffing up its body.

stimuli things from the outside, such as loud noises or bright lights, that make living things react

Living things reproduce

All living things reproduce. This means they make more of themselves. People and some animals have babies by giving birth to live young. Other animals lay eggs.

Crocodiles hatch from eggs.

Most plants grow from seeds. Some plants grow from a cutting. This means a piece of the plant is cut off and planted in soil. The cutting grows into a new plant.

Many plants grow from seeds.

Living things need energy

All living things need energy. They get energy by taking in **nutrients**. People and animals get nutrients from the foods they eat. Most plants get nutrients from the soil they grow in.

Animals get nutrients from food.

Living things die

All living things die. Some only live for a short time. The adult mayfly is only alive for half an hour to one day. Some living things, such as big redwood trees, can live for thousands of years.

nutrients things a living thing needs to grow and heal

Breakaway tasks

Remembering

1 List three characteristics of a living thing and three characteristics of a non-living thing.

2 Tell a partner what you know about living things.

3 Choose five new words from the text and write a glossary.

Understanding

4 Choose an animal and a plant. List three differences and three things that are the same about them.

5 Explain why an apple tree is a living thing.

Applying

6 Use a magnifying glass to look at things from nature, such as a leaf or a feather. Draw what you see.

Analysing

7 Write a checklist to help you decide if something is living or non-living.

8 Prepare a presentation about the characteristics shared by all living things.

Evaluating

9 Decide whether the following things are living or non-living: smoke, mushroom, volcano, kangaroo, worm, rain, gum tree, moth. Explain each decision.

Creating

10 Plan an excursion for your class to help you learn about living things. Where would you go? Why?

Life cycle of a dragonfly

Living things begin their life, then grow and reproduce. This is called a life cycle. Here is the life cycle of a dragonfly.

An adult dragonfly

The dragonfly lays eggs on or near water.

A **nymph** hatches. Nymphs have no wings. They live under water until ready to become an adult.

The nymph leaves the water and climbs up a plant. An adult dragonfly then climbs out of the nymph. It leaves behind its old skin.

nymph a young insect that has hatched from its egg

Breakaway tasks

Remembering

1 Describe each stage of a dragonfly's life cycle.

2 Explain why water is important to the dragonfly's life cycle.

Understanding

3 Explain how a nymph becomes a dragonfly.

4 Research the life cycle of a dragonfly. Write and deliver a speech about it.

5 Write three differences between a nymph and a dragonfly.

Applying

6 Write five true or false sentences for a quiz on dragonflies. Ask a classmate to do your quiz.

7 Find out about another animal's life cycle. Write four facts about what you find out.

Analysing

8 Choose an animal (for example, a frog, a butterfly or a dog) and compare its life cycle to the life cycle of a dragonfly. Are the life cycles similar or different?

Evaluating

9 Research and list dangers to the dragonfly at each stage of its life cycle. Explain which stage is the safest.

Creating

10 Write and illustrate a story about the life of a dragonfly.

Tigers in trouble!

By N. Danger

The Siberian tiger is endangered. There are only about 400 Siberian tigers living in the wild. We must save the Siberian tiger or it will be gone forever.

Danger in the wild

The Siberian tiger lives in cold, frozen forests in Asia. Over the years, the number of tigers in the wild has dropped.

Some people hunt tigers. They sell their skins and body parts.

Some people believe that wearing tiger skin shows they are rich. Some people use tiger bones, teeth, claws and **internal** parts to make medicines. They believe these medicines can cure diseases.

Did you know?
The Siberian tiger is the biggest cat in the world.

internal something that is inside. For example, the heart and lungs are internal – they are inside the body

Habitat destroyed

Siberian tigers are losing their homes. Their forests are being cut down. The wood from the forest trees is used to make paper and furniture.

But some people are fighting to save the Siberian tiger. They are doing this by:

- telling people that tigers are endangered
- changing people's ideas about using tiger products
- asking governments to make laws to stop people hunting tigers
- using less wood and recycling more.

If all these things happen, the Siberian tiger might be saved.

Did you know?
There is roughly the same number of Siberian tigers living in zoos and nature parks as there is in the wild.

Logging can destroy important habitats.

Breakaway tasks

Remembering

1 How many Siberian tigers are left in the wild?

2 How do some people use tiger products?

Understanding

3 Explain why Siberian tigers are endangered.

4 Do you think we should try to save Siberian tigers from extinction? Why? Prepare a speech.

Applying

5 Make a poster that tells others about Siberian tigers.

6 Write a cinquain poem about the Siberian tiger.

Analysing

7 What do you think the author's opinion is about Siberian tigers? Why do you think this?

8 Tiger products should be used to make medicines. Write three points for this argument and three points against this argument.

Evaluating

9 On a scale of 1 to 10, rate how well the author persuaded you to help the Siberian tiger. Give reasons for your rating.

Creating

10 Create a radio advertisement about saving the Siberian tiger.

The Waterhole

By Graeme Base

Down to the secret waterhole
the animals all come,
As seasons **bring forth** drought
and flood, they gather there as one.
United in their common need, their numbers
swell to ten,
But hidden deep amongst the trees lie ten times
that again!
One rhino drinking at the waterhole.
'Snort, splosh!'
...
Two tigers lapping at the waterhole.
'Grrrrr!' ...
Three toucans squawking around the waterhole.
'Ark, ark! Arrrk!' ...
But something was happening ...
Four snow leopards gazing at the waterhole.
'Prrrrrrr.' ...

bring forth to cause something to begin
united joined
swell grow

The pool was getting smaller …
Five moose wallowing in the waterhole.
'Moo, moo, mooooooooiii!' …
… and smaller …
Six catfish **floundering** in the waterhole.
… and smaller.
Seven pandas sipping at the waterhole.
'Tsk, tsk, tsk.' …
Eight ladybirds meeting at the waterhole.
'Bzui.' …
Nine tortoises **lumbering** around the waterhole.
'Scrmph, scrmph, scrmph.' …
Ten kangaroos looking at the waterhole.
There was nothing to say
The water was all gone.
And all the animals went away.
Then a shadow fell across the sun.
Clouds began to gather.
A single drop of rain fell.
It rained and rained and rained and rained …
And all the animals came back!
'Ooola! Oooya! Wahoooo!'

floundering flapping
lumbering walking heavily and slowly

Breakaway tasks

Remembering

1 How many kangaroos came to the waterhole?

2 List the names of the animals in the story in alphabetical order.

Understanding

3 Write a summary of what happened in the story.

4 How many animals in total came to the waterhole? How did you work this out?

5 Why did all the animals come to the waterhole?

Applying

6 Find out which part of the world each animal comes from. Present this information on a chart.

7 Why did the waterhole dry up? How did it fill up again? Answer by drawing labelled pictures.

Analysing

8 What message or messages do you think the author wants to get across by writing this story?

Evaluating

9 This story has a happy ending. How could the story have ended if it did not rain? What does this tell you about nature?

Creating

10 Draw a new animal by putting parts of different animals together. Give your animal a name.

Strands in action

Core tasks

1 Create a 'habitat' diorama.
- Research a habitat, such as a rock pool.
- List the living and non-living things.
- Use craft and natural materials to create a diorama.

2 Create a TV ad telling people why they should look after natural environments.
- List three reasons why people should look after natural environments and three things they can do.
- Write a script for your TV ad.
- Practise your ad, then have a friend film you.

Extra tasks

1 Choose two living things that are similar. List three reasons why they can be grouped together. Repeat with two non-living things.

2 'Endangered animals should be protected.' Do you agree or disagree? Give reasons why.

3 Finish this sentence: 'Living things are different to non-living things because ...'. Use dot points to give at least five responses.

4 Research a living thing that is too small to be seen. Write a report about what makes it a living thing.

With factual texts, it is important to get your facts right. When researching information, always check your facts from two or more reliable sources.